Drafts 15 – XXX, The Fold

Rachel Blau DuPlessis

Potes & Poets Press, Inc.
Elmwood, Connecticut 1997

Potes & Poets Press, Inc.
181 Edgemont Avenue
Elmwood, CT, 06110-1005, U.S.A.

10 9 8 7 6 5 4 3 2 1

FIRST EDITION
Copyright © Rachel Blau DuPlessis, 1997
All rights reserved

Potes & Poets Press thanks The Fund for Poetry for a grant used to assist the cost of the publication of this book.

Cover design: Rachel Blau DuPlessis
Cover prepared by Bob Hunt
Typesetting: Barbara Campbell

ISBN 0-937013-65-x

Printed in the United States of America

Acknowledgements

I should like to thank The Fund for Poetry for a spirit-sustaining grant in December 1993. The Drafts in this book join the series of autonomous, but interdependent canto-like poems on which I have been engaged since 1985-86. The pre-Drafts work, called "Writing" (1984-85), and the first two Drafts were published in *Tabula Rosa* in 1987, and *Drafts 3-14* was published in 1991, both from Potes & Poets Press. Hence I have a great indebtedness to Peter Ganick, the publisher of Potes & Poets. The French translation of several of the Drafts, called *Essais: Quatre Poèmes* appeared with Un Bureau sur l'Atlantique, Editions Créaphis in 1996, translated by Jean-Paul Auxeméry and the translation collective of Royaumont.

These works (sometimes in slightly different form) were originally published as follows:

"Draft 15: Little" (then numbered Draft 16), "Draft 16: Title" (then numbered Draft 15), "Draft 17: Unnamed," and "Draft 18: Traduction," *Sulfur* 32 (Spring 1993). "Little" was chosen for inclusion in *The Gertrude Stein Awards in Innovative North American Poetry: 1993-1994*. "Draft 19: Working Conditions," *Hot Bird Mfg* 11, number 14 (October 1993). It was reprinted in the Mexican journal *Mandorla 4: Nueva Escritura de las Américas/ New Writing from the Americas* (1995). "Draft 20: Incipit," *Parataxis* 6 (Spring 1994). "Draft 21: Cardinals," *Chelsea* 57 (Winter 1994). "Draft 22: Philadelphia Wireman," *Hambone* (Spring 1995). "Draft 23: Findings." Sections published in *Common Knowledge*, *Sulfur*, *The Capilano Review*. and *Lower Limit Speech* in 1995 and 1996. "Draft 24: Gap." *Grand Street* (Fall 1995). "Draft 25: Segno." *West Coast Line* 17 (Fall 1995). "Draft 26: M-m-ry." *The Iowa Review* (Fall 1996). "Draft 27: Athwart," *Poetry New York* (1996). "Draft 29: Intellectual Autobiography." *Chain* 3 (Spring 1996).

With many thanks to the editors of these journals, including Ray di Palma, Clayton Eshleman, Barbara Guest, Burt Kimmelman, Nathaniel Mackey, Douglas Messerli, Roy Miki, Drew Milne, Adalaide Morris, Aldon Nielsen, Jena Osman, Belle Randall, Bob Sherrin, Juliana Spahr, Jean Stein and Roberto Tejada.

Contents

Draft 15: Little	1
Draft 16: Title	4
Draft 17: Unnamed	9
Draft 18: Traduction	14
Draft 19: Working Conditions	20
Draft 20: Incipit	28
Draft 21: Cardinals	32
Draft 22: Philadelphia Wireman	38
Draft 23: Findings	42
Draft 24: Gap	54
Draft 25: Segno	58
Draft 26: M-m-ry	62
Draft 27: Athwart	65
Draft 28: Facing Pages	69
Draft 29: Intellectual Autobiography	74
Draft XXX: Fosse	81
Notes to the poems	87

Draft 15: Little

More than that is hard to say.
I am drawing a blank.

High clouds, their errancy, ply over ply,
    float.
    And still
I float on eddies in a rocking enormity.

Not mourning, not pleasure,
but auras of evanescence,
and nickname-painted train stops,
and jerry-built victrolas,
canoes pulling away sloppily from simple docks
dribble and bonk of paddle,
a particular grab of grasses,
hairy stems of weeds,
and the afikomen so well hidden
plus misunderstood
it was never teased forth.
Never then redeemed.

So I saw what I saw,
like photographs of the war,
stripes under wire,
shadows scummed or smudged on pavement,
and starved locked rows.

Some clocks stopped but not
other clocks, tick and tock and
I was part of all that it,
a lucky nothing
not in the way of particular harm,
half witness half witless
      dot—a little
      yod or yid
amid the clamors of dawn,
waking inside the whiteness,
before anything is given——-
that is, taken.

To this magic table
spread with glistening nap,
a place like a fairy tale: dolorous and lyric,
"un couvert" where the bread is perfect,
dishes, bodies, fruit piled,
cute mugs caffine-coated,
wine in dregs and lees,
and salty bowls of weeds,

there is someone, step, step:
over the bridge, down the field,
under the fence, through the door,
and speaks.

The order is "Take cover!"
And hands to necks
the cowering shapes
wedge under desks
puppets of puppets.

Wherein at play
the smallest chancy jot of scratched substance
bounces along a pebbly day.

Recently I lost my watch
dropped straight down off my wrist
and fell into a hole so far it wasn't there.
Strange,
that litmus wristlet π
had covered my nakedness
and now I was exposed.
Or dreamed I'd "missed my stop."

From that point, those points, on,
the trace or shard, the thing
come passing darkly cross me
in the tunnel dirt of time
was mine.

Not hero, not polis, not story, but it.
    It multiplied.
    It engulfing.
    It excessive.
"It" like X that marks the spot, that is, the spots,
an ever wily while, a wilderness of hope.
The spot of almost hopeless hope.
Can barely credit it.

Thus my voice is empty, but I speak and sing
only of this.
The undersentences
that rise, tides of sediment, the little
stuff agglutinating in time, debris
    I sing.
    Cano,
cannot not do it so.

In time's deep well,
my shallow heart has flooded.

From the exile woods
on the edge of the edge
a little mite doth blow.
A Mite! I might
have killed such mites and bits
    before
    today
I didn't think

of needing such
a Little Mite,
this dusty road.

May 1992–December 1992

Draft 16: Title

A wax nipple,
    a simulacrum nipple
        lodged in the slab of a ledger,
the nipple stark
    as a title
        the fusion sealed
            ardor.
    The whole riveted to the wall.

Each ledger, for there were a number,
    pulled from the abandoned worksite
        presented an unreckoned order, nipple by nipple,
with the tooled faux-leather corners,
    small shutter scenes, a kind of snap-shut
        shot with 4 black corners, and the faces
so small, too small,
    unrealizable, that one could, so far as
        memoir (or saying anything)
goes, say *the same things over and over*
    time and again, various ways.

Yet time is cast off, cast forth.
    Fleeting *beyond one's wildest dreams*
        The arc of a cigarette butt flicked
out of the moving car in front of mine.
    Even the loss is lost.
        "I am borne darkly, fearfully, afar."

My armada of days taken afloat,
    patient, kicking, counting
        the free-style strokes
up and down the pool,
    but the total unaccountable;
        even into extended telling
consumed, never entitled.
    The whole notion of eating:
        eating, eating everything, to get
to the one thing
    that is revealed, an
        avatar of

    the poem, which began by being
        organized loosely, but
            here concerns blood creatures.
Avaler,
    a foreign word to say
        gorge on the body of the dead.

So anyway
    "blurred and breathless,"
        the mottled surface of a mortal body
        wasted away.

The sparking arc of a smoked-to-the-filter butt.
    The careful kick, stroke, breathe of the crawl.
        Silences of water.
Cranky bile, books
    like solemn boobies
        bolted to the wall.

A little variety, please,
muthoplokon!
so one may be thrown,
wrestled to the ground limb over limb and,
by the muthe-plucker,
knotted in holds
hobbling folds
over and beyond the bearable.

Thus the panic over the missing codine, and how,
from that motel, a final short trip
to the middle of nowhere,
could scare up
a prescription of such densities and extensives
that perk and succor
the failing one-breasted body,
a sugar tit of honey suck
one gives the dying—who
could be called?
who, called, could credit
the accident of forgetting.

Just actions, and inadequate summaries:
opening a sealed grim house,
one person in her shallow entry,
that smoky smell of an old motel,
"cottage," "pottage," dank, dark, mildewed.

Yet all that got uttered was
what yard sale and whence
those unfamiliar relics
out of other families' tents—
the flowered butter dish just
slightly cracked,
ancient cameras leaking light—
emerge into unreckonable clutter
at the opening of our tomb.

And "here" the dead with gabble and gargle
pluck sinews one by one, and twist
the terrible tendons to tune
that thrown and fallen pile of flesh
taut as a lyre.

Something will be coming,
some sorry sound.
Of oldest instruments.
But who could credit
such scream, such stream
unsweetened,
thick with unspoken
and unspeakable chords
in the sweet milk of light.

So avaler sa langue, is the expression.
Eat up, swallow, stifle the tongue.
Kashe und shayle.
Questions, more questions,
phantom and evanescent whisps
that evaporate, as if
ashen syllables of Yiddish.

Remember, remember,
remember nothing, but more
than you want to
because following the thread of any one slide
entangles labyrinths
requiring
the rest of your born days
to eviscerate.

A cigarette butt smoking arc'd out a car window,
driver's side puff on the asphalt a series
of dots and disconnections
fire sparks run over
by the next car, the wheels
that ran over the cigarette
of the previous smoker; and the dark car running behind
over the sparky flare
sees it, rolling down the road a little gust,
and then extinguished. Nothing more to find.
Except maybe the unquenchable filter, the threads,
neo-asbestos or polyester,
that catch and muffle, and, finally, fray
in the dump ditch
at the edge of the roadway.

You know the way the cello is so vibrant, and the
piano too,
densities and sonorities that pitch past us
playing hard ball? a shower of desultory fire?

So imagine taking that wood and
slamming it: bam.
Col legno.
What composers in their demonic sweetness
call "extended techniques."

Well, "bam bam bam"
the fist chops the page.
The sound is hardly as convincing
as slugging the cello, gets only a little
rattle, but the gesture———

poetry, schmoetry, it's
dark spurts—it's
words cooked in their own ink:
in su tinta,
which is the creature's blood.

I fall to the tarmac,
filled to the sick.

Given the wrestled
tentacles tendered for food,
given this sauce,
what meat am I eating?
what dark blood letting?
Why this remembering
and that forgetting?
What rears and spurts and thickens
in the fosse?

———————

Now that I'm here,

I'm here.

I'd recognize this place anywhere.

November 1991–December 1992

Draft 17: Unnamed

It's true that every ending only erases the board
rather than filling it.
The poems are written in strange chalk
strange, a chalk
in some lights dark, plump with serifs
on a scumbled, agitated whiteness,
but mainly a white chalk on a whiter page.

Which can hardly be read
and that, only under angled light.

As wide as my life though when you look again it's
a scroll narrow, but fast,
paper towels in the hands of a toddler,
down and up hillocks and rises,
blazes and falls
so fast one can only
trail after it, "what could be more natural."

Or dark as a mist
hanging over the fill-built airport
smoke brown, the sky looks daubed
and of no depth.

But the chalk (with luck, another turn) turns
    translucent, light on light
        which is, in certain lights, like dark on dark
but more
    blinding.

Words,
    scattered falling
        arcs of shame,
            glaze the flicker-ridden labyrinth—
it makes a peculiar medium.
        And its crossgrained nourishment
            demands a strange tooth.

Perhaps translucence is a quality of erasure.
The thing anyway looks like a Cy Twombly
strokes trailing each other and dibs, nibs,
flicks of the wrist and a dreamy evisceration of pencil.
A morning glory bolted across the door.
My little valise is filled with souvenirs.
And none of them is "art."
I can see why he said I wasn't interested in art.

"Poetry depersonalizes 'days'
in language." It sounded
as if this were what I wanted

yet the hole, the sufferance
fell open. Heard the shaped scream of a duration.
Three times: the same, the same, the same again,
"nothing but these facts and all these facts."
Why did he think I "wasn't interested in art"?

Low song clouds in unbelonging places
        emphasize the activities of light,
                which is unspeakable.

While the sound, not just the light,
        plays along certain vectors
                pools in the force field

large, square, rent, timeless
        void. Know?
                Can barely know what labyrinth.

The grass clods push up
        between the lines and cracks
                of pavement. In the depth

of night, a street lamp
        looming behind them
                they rise and lurk,

turf tufts made near twice
        their "real" size
                by shadow.

But what I meant is this.
>   *She stood at the pit*
>   *where, this 50 years,*

155 Jews were shot.
>   *There, near a field of rye,*
>   *she'd found dozens of notes and addresses*

tossed away
>   *moments before their deaths.*
>   *To this day,*

she regrets
>   *that, out of fear,*
>   *she did not pick them up.*

The poetics seems plain.
>   Since then
>   there are many people spend their time

picking up the notes.
>   But they are not there.
>   They are as gone as possible to be.

So the gathering
>   is impossible.
>   But still the shapes are bowed,

and search
>   this otherwhere of here.
>   Yet had they actually

been there
>   that time
>   being remembered,

it is equally possible
>   they too would have left
>   all of them where they lay.

What illusion, what delusion, what disillusion
>   writes these gaps?
>   tries these missing bits and scraps?

It is not elegy
    though elegy seems the nearest category of genre
        raising stars, strewing flowers. . . .

It's not that I have not
    done this, in life or whereever I
        needed to

or throwing out the curled tough leather
    of the dead
        the cracked insteps of unwalkable shoes,

but it is not the name or term
    for what is meant
        by this inexorable bending.

And it is not "the Jews"
    (though of course it's the Jews),
        but Jews as an iterated sign of this site.

Words with (to all intents and purposes)
no before and after
hanging in a void of loss
the slow and normal whirlwind
from which it roars
they had not ever meant to be so lost,
so little wordth.

                There are plenty of reasons to wonder.
          Forlorn spirits with spinning "swords of flame"
                    as much like angels
                 as it's possible to be, but without
               choices or pleasure, stand empty.
                    Wavy wheaty heads
                         dart and sway;
           contradictory rages swivel them.
               But (pace Rilke) we can tell
             these angels, or their similacra
                          "things."
      Late busses, glass smash, styrofoam containers.
                    Low sun plain wing
                         grey toyota
                            ormolu

                              soccer freshener
                                    kith, soot,
                                          food,
                               rainbows of oil.

                              The intersection
                                    by Dunkin'
                              Donuts, chicken
                                buckets, milk
                                 and Gulf is
                          where you have to turn

                                         coming
                                          here.

So speak, stutterer, and stain the light with figments.
    Rush, and brush, this evanescent shimmer
              that does not even track

that does not
     even fill or replicate
              the historical air clotted here.

And Here
     where all this is and are,
              this back and forth through time,
Alight.
     It's never
              what you think.

                                May–December 1992

Draft 18: Traduction

Pas tout à fait cela.
    Not quite it?
        It's not exactly that
that A
our edge of it
billows before us.

useless, cannot quite grasp . . .

be little spot, be draft of
changes,
litmus ribbons
        strips blowing, situés
        roses et bleus,
        flicker . . .

face aux grands enjeux du siècle.

B
Something: an extract or essence of something
else; this work pressed onto itself
enfolded imprint,
sleep-writing on a blanketed body . . .

Words stranger even to themselves
than cryptograms, like le
or it, ce/ça or see/saw,
always with an inside out, an outside in,
a sound, a toss,
et la Syntaxe étrange, d'étrangère

to suggest shades

of the unspeakable

Iota. These fragments "conspicuous

oracles"

cast off on the silence. . .

C —a task
assuming an exile
of, and in, the world.
Writing defined as
seeing or being
between, for even in one's ownèd language
can see it as translation,
not of text, but of
interstices, blank or overlooked, rough
muddy spots which dogs pee up
this common tuft or
that a black comb was pressed down into asphalt
when all this was repaved,
odd corner, or

if not translation
writing as foreign
from the very first.

Finally, D.
Under the quiet umbra
of the midnight sky a-wait.

The shadow waxing
wonderful to watch,
at once so slow and fast
across the moon.

Yet watching the eclipse I began champing
impatiently. Type A in R.
Taxed by waiting, even in wonder.

To hope any micro-moment will
speed itself forward to the next only accelerates
that whole which goes this fast
and faster still,
this speck, of life. . . .

During which the dark shape
of what we're living on
passes above us,
Galactal smudge.
It's earth. E.

It's where we are,
the wonder is.

Ainsi (A, B, C, D, Etc.) les questions de
traduction se lancent
leurs plaintes silencieuses.

A is for A.
Each thorn and eth,
wirds
you've never seen be-for-
weirds,

        Grandes ampoules
        de plastique
        à moité flottant dans les eaux mortes des canaux
        objets d'ard, comme a dit Duchamp,
        are swamped.

        Chestnuts, gravel, chestnuts
        semés parmi les cailloux, impossible
        pleasures, crushed.
        C'est marron.
        C'est génial.

All these words have to go into another language;
toute proportion guardée,
where does it mean they "go"?

Go somewhere, that is all.
Go elsewhere
round the dusky dome of time.
Passing over each other, eclipsing light with dark
and dark shimmering with strangeness
so we look, as never be-
fore, at what was
always there—
the inside out of space.

B. Pullulating surges:
scripsi o so
curious and fine.

Ligne de blanc.

Ligne de noir.

League of blank and nor.

Tinier, thicker, denser
than spider webs' wet silver,
blanks and nor—
the text
expressing

un silence, et en plus, un réseau intraduisible
fait comme tissu,

dans lequel quelques JE's et EUX's
se trouvent piégés—
and these
glossalalic trembling wings
snagged in webs of quiet
proposent un spectacle
son-et-mots, un jeu quelconque
where words (mots) bubble, where something
(mut, matte, moot) the mud ferments, and
gets to be another word, mote.

Mote speaking.
Mote spoken.
Bubbles, syllables, galaxies
of babble.

C that C.
A ce moment je mords la langue
quand je rêvais.
Elle est plus large maintenant
que ma bouche.
There are edges and sides
Endges and -cides
it now has it never
had before, it seems

never to have been so large
as now,

swollen, tender, tendus, swilling

LA LANGUE

hard to articulate, slower, but faster
than ever before j'ai passée ces jours
dans une tempête

des petits mots crépitants dont
les expressions ondeuses se font,
auprès desquelles on trouve
au vers
un bon blanc, des vers
qui heurtent
au fond d'un couloir gothique
où des hirondelles en ogive
se nichent juste au croisement
de chaque arc.

I am a black shape moving forward
marging with a black shape
cast like a die upon the stone.

Lettres, j'entre
dans le passage
d'une langue
à une autre,
et de l'autre
à l'outre,
rempli/vide
ici/là
et bien iota/yod.

From all these langu-bytes?
I'm just translating time.

C'Sont des pages noires
avec sidereal speck
a work in hardly any language.
Not of the word, but of the gap.

An experience we are said to have
and the shadow
of experiences we never shall have.
Multiple approximations
of more unstructured, wicked problems.

En plus, E. Etc. It's almost endless
but totally constrained.
It's time, like a path,
littered with the evidence
of nomadic occupation,
these burnished vagaries of use
that I'm after.

I'm after everything, and after nothing.
A belatedness so strong
I come,
even after what is
not there,

after eradication
Who inhabits one's own time

who can be witness
after the eclipse of witness

cannot not speak. O poetry
—again and again no more poetry.

Nothing
is extensive enough
for this level of abandon-
ment,
éminemment macaronique or
marconique, wire-less towers
on a windy shore
transmitting micro-shifts of sound and state-
ment cross a space we do not understand.

"traduire, c'est le contraire"
"de quoi?"

October 1992–January 1993; September 1994

Draft 19: Working Conditions

I.

This kind of speaking
doubles the unspeakable.

With every word
ossuarial shadows.

Come, the gathering. But chancy.
Which randomness is shocking

and may thus motivate more
toward silence than toward speech.

For who can, not silent,
accept the vocation

to acknowledge, to describe,
or even to allow

the enormities

of which one must,
if speaking,

speak.
And the details.

One site cut and recut
twine gridding the sectors of dirt

To have found a grit-filled room
sift gram upon grain

and seek the deep-slung shard
amazing, that any "traces"

once "effaced"
should thereby be "called back."

To have fitted wordless words
inside or over words: for what?

scattered further than dirt,
scattered with atoms, ashes, stars

I live
so in my time

II.

handwriting traces
                            These terms:
                              traces
"have   *effaced*
    (he said) in the inverse order
        been (regularly) called back"
                            and *called back*
(an addled syntax)
with mixed results.

Every word teeming and bereft,
the whole writing
with underspeech parts, incomplete leavings,
offers riddled pockets of unarticulate keens
in shadowy lotteries.

Is then the work lucid and stuttered?
sullied and sullen? startled and studied?
Always, and beyond reproach.

    What's done, is done

and now
                        Because so evanescent
                        because their syntax baffles
                        these words shadow me.

    it must begin again.   The inside-out of space
                      a mass of unthinkable matter
              and its miniscule nobilities,
        a dog, say, jingling her tags—

    there's something she wants, something
simple, something she needs to remind us.

III.

Living within
a place where little noises
in wonder at their own skew
hang in the opening.

Carried cavernous
the politics of our time,
insomnias of rage, join them.

On small page self
rose the giant letter moon.
Time is like a path,
but it works on the principle of flickering.

IV.

She wrote: "nothing
    is ever lost. It will recur,"
        but this I did not

believe. In fact
    I thought it
        ignorance of time.

Resistance
    to this (loss)
        in which we are limed.

So many ways to be lost.
    Can barely count
        the ways.

The condition of work being struggle in time.
    With loss.
        And with these random findings.

I resisted initiations
>   into "virile pieties,"
>   which were everywhere, nevertheless.

But the rage of the mother
>   is an unsolved problem
>   in language.

V.

Tremped in such conditions—
it's like renting a canoe
and suddenly a windstorm
suddenly thunderheads   A lot of "suddenly"
come up on a lack, I got
lack on the page, but it was really lake, a lake
bigger than it seemed,
at first opportunistic
paddle, and
plunk in the middle of turbulent
atmospheres, where it's just a matter of chance.
She said "look down," as if time were readable
layers, and you could get a grip
map   it, it

to me, disturbances are terms. Crosscurrents

cab here, cab there, mirrored taxis
swinging wildly thru traffic
of the dead
in transit, dead
galore, carryovers from one side to the other
zigzag, fizzle and flare, a series of linked bombs,
orange disinfectant scrub for incision
never any operation but
Thunderheads, lightning from the distance,
green shadow, maternal aunt
starved herself down
65 pounds

"living skeleton."
                              Later there will be plenty of
Sounds, the dog in the morning yawning: Owwwww—
we say she has said "out."
                                   the word "nothing."
And what other words were to be said off, set off
and what other transfigurations of letters?

"so i had a feeling tonight that nothing i meant to say was over yet

that it was also too late to start

which led me to think i would start later...."

VI.

rondo
junco
window
any color of any thing could speak of that

plate at the shadowy end of the table, green bites

of things, diverse, flecked thru, ambulant, riven

with "multiphonics, circular singing"

and family life, a courtyard of pebbles, raw walls

from a "typical opening and contrasting idea"

road to road so
enter and immense the muddy byways,
the dark clustering
underside.

Even a documentary only stretches so far.

The "inharmonic sonorities" make
as if a piece of time crossed with place had got
brief speaking consciousness,
but has no pronoun and no shape
—not it, nor she, nor me—
so cannot be referred to.

Cannot via well-ruled poem-wedges,
can only flicker at these phatic edges.

VII.

Though it's true that "it" is

closest to it,
all told,

it
was never what I was ready for any time
it seemed to be happening

belatedly
spurts of moment,

dawn winds
that rush around the earth to

roaring place, and roaring time
while small trim sounds go

peep • peep • peep •

which striates my dust-speck

"not boiling to put pen to paper."

On the page the word "recall"
trick of the eye, I read it as "rachel."
Could not follow the instruction.

And the person also
far to the left, something wrong with the capacity for centering
here
almost off the picture
which otherwise is a rectangular piazza in Sweden
a kind of foreign "emptiness"
reminding not so much of space
but of time
will never return.

VIII.

For disappearance is the subject
    of whatever I do.

If not disappearance,
    then what is here.

"During my long nights with these corpses,
    I understood

that they would accompany me
    till the end of my life."

Even at fair distance
    certain photographs

bulldozed ditches in consciousness
    corpses dump into the seam

corpses jump like trout
    backward and forward in my stream.

Still, much will be forgotten.
    Disappearance,
for instance, of crimes
    done for me.
Cheap whatever
    from a monocrop.
Children's clothing
    factory-stitched by children.

Officialdom
    comparatively cordial.

Utopian space
of anger and connectedness
beyond barrier.
And this is the space can never
talk, but
go to
foraging.

IX.

This is the work
This is the work

Disfigured

Form as experienced

Struggle, over the mark.

And over the effacement

Tangle conflicting
words, undersides, notes,
disappearances.

Those skeins, extended and tightened,
wound so many years,
have ended (once more)
in an unpickable knot.

One simply present: here.
The objective to say: Here is a knot.
No mystery here.
Not in that.

June–August 1993

Draft 20: Incipit

Curious, this querying letter from a stranger.
    Just when I had in fact
turned back to begin,
    it made me think again
where I had been.

Wash of the day, bitterness, and what observation to make?
    how the basic primal

        luck

of having emptiness on this scale

operated. Or occurred.

Blessed, one could say,
    with a bad, with almost no
        memory,
gifted with it,
    the flower was always
        false forget-me-not,
tender blue, very like the real,
    those sugar'd golden-pinky eyes
        but not right, a lack—

something
    of how the texture of memory
        puckers,
slippage.
    It's never what you think.

Something   —   an extract or essence of something else; this work
pressed down   unfinished   overwritten   refolded

iota. That fragments are "conspicuous"
oracles. That the veil of mist behind which stars
shimmer and show
was, in fact, the Milky Way itself, not clouds at all,
    nor close;
That the diasporic

        scattering, scattered even in the "home,"

talmudic
        aura of endlessly welling commentary

folding and looping over
Is.

        Like it.

        IT IS.

And that was it.

It sentenced me for life.

The beginning was, as these things go,
negation. But
'twas also setting forth of signs to read or tell.
Moonlit refraction by a strange heap
counted on base "N" and on base "Y."
Yes and no. Both and and.

And inside that beginning
the no no no set out, unrolled
its grave and merry way,
winding a lane but in a trackless sense
through scudding days, on awe-scratched bumps,
over the design of hills perpetually
blustered with cross-drafts and wind-chills,
spiraling and knotting over itself:
the vulnerable.

Underground, streams of stone
hiss and percolate.
Super-heated gouttes
pop according to the vectors of physics
to form, as they fling,
the drop-pocked texture of time.

It's a cobalt time spent in the wilderness,
ugly lure, and sullen tasteless fish,
guns galore and ready to roll,
which is simply the time here,
time spent observing
small hopes begin the oddities of journey,
time spent hearing
mournful hoots at venomous crossings,
time spent trying
to step step step quivering silver prongs
of struggled tuning.
Time contaminated. Time full of dimension.
Time wrapped in a family of apples.
Time again and time again,
that runs clear out
into the starry randomness of scattered far,
way beyond the articulate limits of syntax.

Pause   space   work   space,   inside emptiness
                    to write is to drown, rip tide, rip time.

Pause work, false work, milky work,
                    time and tide in wait for nomad.

Aged dog, her murky running eye—
                    dawn time, even tide.

Nits and gnats, snits and snats, born for the minimum,
finite, finished, fermished
and dead in a minute,
into the air a little spill
as invisible dust-threads spot shimmering down
and swim in beams of ever-mobile light,
named fixedly, obsessively,
tenderly, "hunger"
to honor who and what we are.

What a joke. What a job

endlessly
to research objects, colors, items, targets, designs
caught in the mottled crossfire of time.

"Those were gunshots huh?"
"Yeah an your dead"
and so they were,
unmistakable,
with a nervy echo.

―――――――

*It's because I ran out
of paper that I'm writing this
on another draft.*

*So here and there
a stranger word
comes through.*

It being the only canvas
wide enough for human sadness.

October 1993–January 1994

Draft 21: Cardinals

N. Letters on familiar matters

Small site:
    inch square cancelled stamp and why
save those pretty timbres from elsewhere, that
    they have been on a journey? and ended? landed?
Letter before the storm
    leaf sides twisting, folded in a thick green light.
Mummified in the eaves, perfect bird
    skeleton, the roofer wanted it and took it.

Taken as literal.
    The small words, written in pain and rage
that marked her latter
    existence. That were its
guarantors. Four lines
    into the inchwide day space
allotted in those calendars,
    Renoir et Cie,
plump with situational irony.
    The unsolved problem, rage
of matter. Pencilled by the livid mother.

        ∧ ∧

The fact that the room, fresh painted, was entirely empty, whilst the house was not, made the room the site of the dream.

Someone flat as paper lies in that room
whose shelves are blank.
A sego lily—white, writ purple in the calyx.
Taboo, tight stairwell.

In the thin space
the maternal tower.

In the window, 2 globes.
The distortion of glazing twins vision

like the strabismic moon you'd see
double-edged, teary-eyed on a windy walk.
Globe upon globe,
the reflection doubles intent.

"But with Schönberg, affability ceases."

An implacable canopic jar
contains the shambles

a broken watch, "can't it be fixed?"

a leaky camera taped, "perhaps valuable"

depression glass:

Plans to elaborate, lost.

∧ ∧

These are, then, ghost pieces.
Dust caught in an indent in the woodwork.
Tie shots of fetish objects. Overlap
of time, a fold in place
as if a camp joke in the prissy pines,
vast once, the dirt path steep, will "always remember"
had said
how muddied with clay the roadrock was.
But now?
What to ask, and of what past, or path.
Some texts conjure memory.
But for N., the continuous negation
of memory in Lethe
is the, albeit intermittent, task.

33

E. Diary of days that may have existed

Waking at dawn to hear the penetrating
rain, rain seeping into time
lavender-grey patches of the changeable
I have become the mourner
somewhat of a change.

∧ ∧

Would you exchange
for this sodden, rusty territory, for
snow tinted with a pink melt chemical
and crusted soot?
For these warming sediments of unfinished business
which settle and then
float again, colloidal, which slide
and toss, which seep and leak
saturated with debris?

Exchange what?

∧ ∧

It's time like a path
littered with items from nomadic
occupation, the burnished vagaries of use.

Yet at every moment one encounters
direction-saturated cardinals
in rose-splayed constellations.

So much, so many, yet, in a cold E. light,
resentful, embattled, and empty.

Stream of nonsciousness, an
emptiness on this scale astonishes,
given that salty pacs
of food engineering
do fill you up.

Articulately sprayed: SO

WHAT THA FUCK

YOU LOOKIN AT?

∧ ∧

"absence of what qualifies this surface?"

There are sublime fields of color.

There are uncountable ranges of failed excess.

It is hard to situate, hard to encompass direction,

call it "true north" or

"true blue," whatever.

What's to find in the woods

anyway? The news says

the body of a woman has been found.

The point of this statement is crude,

like a statement about concrete barrels of dreck

packed "with acquisitions, consolidations,

spinoffs, mergers, and layoffs"

being dumped, with calculation,

deep in the everlasting ocean.

S. The translation of betweenness into betweenness

"'On foot,'" said S.,
"'I had wandered up and wide
thru galaxies and stars
before I'd even plucked
at the loose red thread
of my red, red dress,'

but once I'd picked and pulled
a little play of the side seam,
worrying it, with its unstuck overcast bit,
trying to unravel stitches into thread,
once I had taken that wrinkling thread
and picked and pulled,
and pulled and picked,

I found that constellations
and blood-red sprigs of tensile lint
suffused each other and intertwined.
Once I had tinkered and twisted the red thread round,
once I had attended solar systems with their unfathomable time,
it was cardinal pleasure;
I sought more of the same,
somber surface of one red dwarf,
its lush, atom-laden namelessness,
and red selvedge into the labyrinth."

W. Atlas of the rufous earth

      The biggest disorder of time
is memory's frayed existence;
    "a disorder of memory" is memory itself.
The continuous encyclopedia
    with its categories unformed
its indices unmade
    its alphabets unorganized.

In the backyard, a consistory gathers
    to elect the next moment,
tufted, coral-beaked, doubled doubles.
    Males, bright raccoon on red,
females, some days iridescent
    a pinky greenish brown,
others, a buff, dull, moody fluff.

The point for W. comes down to
being a hinge, constructing oscillations
adequate
to shock and to recurrence,
taking
words from before, words from after;
replaying
for new pleasures of preposition
words
that never were from anywhere, yet
form place
irresistably, and further, at the site of repetition,
form changes.

                ∧ ∧

It's 4:32 exactly.
A terrible dream, but one
not impossible now for girls of ten:
"bad people coming into the house"
and will not wake to tell what happens then.

Here and there, day and night I walk out into
the least particle of astonishment
in which nourishment collects.

But whatever there is to say,
    a vibrato among the cardinals
        splits words at the point of their affirmation
            casting the bits adrift in syntax
                half in and half outside the compass of silence.

May 3, 1993–May 23, 1994

Draft 22: Philadelphia Wireman

Red "8" dreamscrip double
travelling red "8" inside the train; these twists *are twinned, are*
tricky tracks following the trail of any conjuncture, fused in the yard
where signals web, and spoked electricity
         spooks furrows, making kaolin

        the moon. HOW, what is this HOW
by silverleaden street lamps,   ordinary site,
that debris insomnia   topographic extreme, cool lit   MADE.
Spurts and flecks of dirt along the baseboard. Red number shadow
                                  registers neon fizz.
            Twisted together
     scratch, gum, mite, dust, web
        agendas; the overspill
              exilic.
Possessed forsaken bridges
      asymmetrically, wherever   *debris insomnia* trebled

                               ordinary stuff
          extreme, cool lit
Juncted *agendas* that twine their *hinge*

scratch, gum, mite, dust: travelling   the range of signs.
      Grunge things junk things, things singed by light.
      HOW hung the hinge from void to word
from word to work   the rage *of signs*
      from work to bode   *asymmetrically*
                      wherever *agendas* TRAVELLED.
   The detritus
lucking the traumscrapt: lucking
            transcript, trauma, script, and scrap. How scraped down to
radiobones—*spurts and flecks* of awe, and joy-
      rigged jerrybuilt trash dense ovoids   zig-filled zeros
          forsaken bridges:
      So much for structure, triple,
  odelike, but *twisted together, fused*
      the same, the same, the same again.

Had wound already *radio* - text—hinging welds
for reels and rolls of silver. Ratiocinated lap joint. Lapis.
Foldit the wire. Foaled OF.
Did OF again.
Heard the mixing of the tracks   *red "8" inside the train*
did mop microchip matting more and more
from woof to bode. Did lapsed card, bent
pin, phillips screw, pop top, junk spot, knurled nut,
and plastic stirrer down by the loading dock.

HOW, what made from Cars, acceleration, crushed cans *Who*
heard the mixing of the tracks and chose to shunt the folded twist

that
wires systems, that cycles cyclonic light. WHO MADE
chromatic models impossible *webbed* down in the rest
who circulated zigzag workings   *filled zeros.*
WHO DID the work?

Clusters of electricity and notation
from the dump ditch
but mum's the word.

Glisten of bright glass bits
thru the work dirt, making, of
green and white wire, of silver wire
voracity part of terror
of thick brown electric cording:

In signage and binding
work the working
in budgets of mismatched numbers
colored rubber bands wrapped, and *OF AGAIN*
wrapped this, wrapped this, wrapped this
mummy
of wattage,
wire wadding inside TV backs crushed and matched.

Raygun downtime wire
wound round talisman. *Can you tie*
Hard store spiky columnmojo
talismum   circulations
of wrapping.

39

Bottle-cap, bracelet, bundled scrap, conductor wire
tape ribbon   condensed ballast   erased ballads *travelling the rage*
of signs.

Wrapped this, wrapped this, wrapped this, wrapped this
in the upbuilded.
Allegro, largo, presto, dominato, and elegy.
Cifar, naam, vak, datum, klas,
plastic, glass, package, trademark, umbrella,
batteries, pen, leather, reflector shatter,
cellophane, spring spirals, filigree naturewire,
cap nut, square nut, wing nut, lug,
bolts and clamps, telephone listings, bulb sprok,
nails, foil, coins, toys, watch,
tools, trinkets, tickets
AND quivering filament.

Can you tie up Spirit Writing *the hinge from void to word to work*
on the wadded page randomize the flow of paths.
DO bottle-cap talism-
um ur flicker inside the upbuilded. Be *in the OF*
and MAKE deep spurts from depths of cursive scrimmage.

Electrodynamic powered surge. *Can you tie*
up round bent,   wicked wrinkled
wrung out, folded up
time to do it
in.
Stroked electricity. *Chromatic*
conjunctures hingeknob crushed
HERE. and HOW.
Cans glittery sharp. Spilling onto the street.
Flicker inside the upbuilded
bits. *Foldit* matter
dreckbundle wireloaf static mingled whirlwind
wound whorl work.
Street light greeny-silver
glittery sharp. Play "8."

40 greyish watts across the way. *Can you*
pin to place ELECTRIC
websaw system, *tie*
IT   from the square-law curve of light,

mark another point OF, dots,   *can you tie*
flicker and hiss, neon spark rune *can you tie up*
> *the anger*
> *of the dead?*

March 1994–August 1994

Draft 23: Findings

1. Pretty difficult to say, finally,
if it's loss or gain that is the subject; they are so
mingled, as
> someone sleeping is mingled up, in it
without knowing it.
A tangle of night sweats

> maybe falling,
> on edge.
> This could be the finding.

>> Penis wiles, link and unlink.

>> Small hot moon
>> now set.

2. Possible to say
"it was shot hand-held."
Just so—jerky, as they ran or fell,
something about the film speed
which exaggerated rhythms: took it slow
and played it fast.

Splots of meta-light on the old film—
an empty celluloid flash streaks the picture
randomly,
and light is even more ambiguous
in the dream.
Because one cannot say from what source or space
that beamy dream light streams.

> quietly over a misted lake
> feathering oars.
> Angelic.
> And J? does that interlocutor
> stumble over the hard-bit shingle?
> squeamishly slog thru
> lake-compost up to the ankles
> just to get "in" to begin with?

3. Delivered
came a ghost letter, typed, but not with ribbon,
so only the pressure of letters
was left, white incised, take a look, it's in
long paragraphs, but the sheet solid blankness;
and beyond "hard to read," erasing its palpability,
and beyond the fact
it is impossible to read at such length
inside a dream is
seeing a glimpse of what forever
could be of
words, but was in fact words never.
Yet even losing it as I skimmed
and the insult of loss shadowing
my ebbing tries, still I looked forward then
now to decipher this token of care, wanted
badly
to read it, meaning to me
so much that it had come thru the mail,
a corresponding letter, but without black letters on it,
so black to blank it went unrolling back,
with the
"in" from invisible,
the deeper double "in" and "in" from finding
and made a dissolve.

Thus the message was lost, yet
an atmosphere enveloped this space from now to not
from not to knot and non- and back and forth
to now
in which the letter opened and declared
(direction indeterminate)
what it was, and what it was to be.
Signed,
in his inimitable handwriting,

Lee

4. I am not in it at all.
All the shadowy interlocutors await the setting down
of any mark.
They will jump

stark in the crevices of dailiness.
The prying, the twisting, riddle and edges suddenly being
moved to rigor, tears, astonishment, rage, luminosity. These
can barely be organized "in"
anything. Washes of color across time? Ebb,
flow, and lee? Pictures of so-called
"things" (a rock, a boat, a gnarled bush) floating
across enormous scrolls
whose creamy whiteness is made to stand for
mist and mist and still more mist, in which
nothing, essentially, is visible?

Given: a week, the original cluster of seven wanderers, one day
after another, this and that "lyrical diary";
Given: a multiple of weeks, a pocky
twenty-eight blaze lunar path;
Given: an alphabet in twenty-six;
or Postulate the twenty-four
planetary hours, each invested by a chronocrator,
"the Angel or the Power that rules this hour," with no telling
what schemes,
or Propose a finite number of random things, which have nonethless,
as sorts sorting,
fallen just so for now:

and by coincidence, for it is 4:32 exactly,
darkly.
Delicate, the digital descent of three simple numbers.

5.   So. These pinholes.

Hear the wind.

      This instruction—without question—

as clear as it needs be.

6.   Rusty fungi, lichen-sided trees, grainy granite,
dots in time
which one could gloss over and over

from the vulnerable dissolve
from the waking discharge of darkness
from there to here—an old measure of holding.

It's as if the whole is an ark
everything doubled, adrift, and
overshooting landmark.

Moved speechless. Between each word
there is such space, whole years to the day
prolix nekeuia,

To the day itself, to the very day in which awakening
blue estate, fourth wall, there are attested facts,
tinny whisperings stating time, news, accidents.

7.   A bird plate,
a bone-handled knife,
a cow mug,
tender things,
inventorying just
those special to here.

All unevenness and yelling up
and down stairs—what
message—sneakers—come on!
A dashing road—
being on it, nothing
too small—red line, three dollars, egg bagel,
sock hole, pattern whine, chipped glass.
That loop in time between "hurrying"
and "postponed"
which is now.

8.   For filaments
already spun, hang, hung and
were already blown and flung
billowing junctures
from roof to plant, from chair to car
to porch, tree, pail, table, and bush,
multiples that cannot

attach the points there are
however many hypotenuses
one postulates, that go cross every X
and every T, that triangulate
even things one cannot even note.

9.   Dance, accepting a good deal of dancer sound.
Squeaks, wet pants, huffing the beat, and spin.
Take talismans, pilgrim, and lay them
invitingly across the blank
white-black mine in which light holding my hands so

touchingly in one arc throw the die into time
the spotty body falling by chance, and again, bet.

That's how I walk.
That's how I talk.
O baby, that's what I like.

10.   Entering under the lintel of the alphabet
in the epistolary mode
I write with letters in letters, and
the correspondence intensifies
from one to one.
Some texts conjure memory one full day.
But the restraint of the rememberer
is so bold that fissures and fragments
compete with finish.
What "little" epic monuments?
What "flash" lyric memory?
What mazy feminine boxhedge, trained so?
What mythic press is this?
What struggle to escape?
Why am I so hard on poetry?

The trail is broken, and the sound skein
loosened and tightened
threads an unpredictable way.
Orion way off around, and under
below the west, has turned, as a matter of course,
since November, and his enormous X,

the fuzzy clutch of sisters at his belt,
and the strong corner stars shining eons of vibrato
are folded away for now.

A milk seed blowing, thus contrite the rememberancer
considers the milky baby-hairs of time.

11. Wet rails, and the oil of crushed leaves.

Forget sententia.

Just a button by the curb.

That extremity dilates vision, I can barely
walk where it is, registering
the vectors, its self, its sewer,

its user, its loser,
their possible pattern, to repeat
it (or in) again,

cast into chance, give them odds,
it's all or nothing
with modifications.

Typing loose; getting losse on the page,
to repeat it again.
Is grande randonnée—a walk down a trail—

linked to random? or is it all
sets of linked modules, each logical
only to themselves.

But with the "d" on my keyboard
sticking and "ifficult" to register
because of the sticky weather

I got on the page "linked moules"
which authorizes a double homage
to MM. Marcels Duchamp and Broodthaers.

Absolutely not the same idea as the
zoom in on the button.
In fact, it's totally opposite,

but both are present
never- and
nonetheless.

12. Non. Say it "known," that is "none" as nones and tides
a certain prayerful force.
Say it "non-" — as non-combattant, non-participant,
and fear again, as during the so-called Gulf War
of wearing even a scrap of non-compliance or resistance
because of the ferocious "support"
itself perhaps just support for a "fast action"
and bringing the combattants
home to engulfment in our usual lives.
Now suffering from the deformities of
their recent children,
chronic malaise, nervous system totally shot,
falling apart at the touch,
from inexplicable untracable non-focused or inadmissable
agents inciting
chemical or biological
aceldama-rich damage.

Understand complicity and cowardice.
When little yellow rosettes and flags
are sported in a certain
atmosphere, can barely speak

known, and non- or "non!"
the french for NO
"we should have known"
or said NON!
faster?
Being powerfully sorry
being unspeakably sorry
now, let me count the ways.

48

13. Cricket cages, summer and autumn,
airy or warm, encouraging song.
Tiny cricket-plates for dinner,
porcelain, depicting aphids.
Cricket beds as snug as boxes
cricket poems inscribed inside them,
just the ticket for insect reading.
Cricket rings for bouts of boxing,
and long brush-like cricket teazles
to push them to the ring and make them fight.

14. These quirky manifestations.
Incidents of a time, spare and concise.
Vines rusted to the trestle.
Six hours of sight-lines and
the "and" of Williams.

A capuccino smell.
And more.

You're looking at this space right now.
So put "your basic message" right here.

15. It's a cup, a plate, junk mail,
a dribble from the dog's mouth,
Gettysburg, from the library,
in the Landmark Series,
shin guards, scrap of paper
with raisin bread, blue cheese, and 898-7108 in 215
with multiple arrows vectoring off.
A clothespin moved from here
to there; after five days
it's put away,
the clarity of little occasions
for sorting.

16. That findings be
a kind of renga chain, circulating with oneself.
An in-depth counting.
Still to have said

"moon," "constellation," or "the change to autumn"
enough and in the elegant cycles of association
effortlessly,
is not possible right now.

17. Basement corners, storage, cellar powders
    the accumulation of stuff impasto,
        doors, boards, tubs, wires, ropes, paint, shelving, foldups
interior wasteplaces
    articulation of sliced trim and trash wood, dehumidifier, yes,
        here's stuff plenty handy.
Dark Hill. Iron Stack. First Day Lake.
    and Red Floor, White Floor. These wee keeps
        tenderly of the used,
"at once natural and industrial,
    crude and refined,
        gritty and elegant."
Not quite my findings.
    But, given everything,
        they might as well have been.

18.   Couscous. Arugula. Bulgar. Mango.
Pesto with pine nuts. Tomatoes, basil, oil.
Rosemary. Foccacio. Ratatouille. Capuccino.
Garlic.

Romaine. Danish blue.
Coffee ice cream.
French bread. Apricot jam. Raspberry seltzer.
Carrots. Turmeric, fenugreek, cloves.
Seltzer with lime.
Garlic.

Bagels. Saga blue. Goat.
Olive oil. Frying peppers and feta.
Salmon. Chicory and Boston. Arugula.
Cannelli, sage, and garlic.
Pasta. Pesto with walnuts.
And garlic.

Locatelli. Canteloupe. Salsa on jimaca.
Corn chips.
Jersey tomatoes,
basil and olive oil. Sour dough. Penne.
White from Orvieto.

Arugula, zucchini, broccoli rabe,
granny smiths, spinach fettucini,
green beans with soy sauce,
vanilla yogurt, croissants, strawberry jam,
and garlic.

Bananas. Greengage.
Black. Italian prune. Wheat pilaf.
Trout au bleu.
Watercress.

Capuccino. Capuccino. Capuccino.
Fresh lemonade.
And garlic.

19.   The qwerty keyboard was invented
to slow the typist down
so the individual letters
would not clump and jam.

It bears no resemblance, as you intuited,
to the frequency of letters used in English.

And your funny writing—
well, Mommy, you have
unreadable writing too:
look at that "ing"; it looks like a "y."

20.   Through the light, a glisten and shining
the streaks' diffusion intense inside the lens,
looking up from textual reproduction
o language, language,
fingers caught in black and white beside the poem.

There is enough to look into
here for the rest of a lifetime
the while whisp whittles of syntax
how to make the language draw

up, across the "contours"
(the way of beginning
as if all over again), these
diaries of hours that may as well have existed.

21. About rhumbs, gradations on the compass rose.

A silent turning in all directions

drawing attention to its shape: circle, vector and box

silence, emptiness, dumb

diminishing, suddenness, fear,

void, gradations, swings,

wind shifts, wind chill, wind shear,

factors, statistical probability, cab brnt, mn ded

flt scttr

look out where.

Boxing, turn that magic wheel, round and round

and random, some spurt, some pulse, some phrase, but what and where:

Could be a particular kind of "R" like a "rho,"

rhapsody, rheum, rhythm, rhododendron, rhyme.

Why here, why this, why now, why me, or no?

That's what I have to say.

The word itself, with its rh- and -umb,

jostles the memory.

22.   Engulfed, each night,
with tsunami from the vibrant void
of sky and space,
from the implacable emptiness, or unfillable fatedness
of all spires, cycles, works, words, worlds, and wires:

Thus. To be so. In is.

23.   The experience of thinking
of one's own absence. Of one's
randomness.
Whatever brought you in
to being, and the little
chances, the accidents
of the living
"missed, but not by much"
"any nearer the artery"
"no helmet, but really lucked out"
"105.9, she was burning up."

Black speckled night,
the generous enchantment of being
in shadowy places,
and hearing whispy contingent
whirlwinds suddenly twist the leaves
of that branch over and over,
inside the unremarked extent of unknowable time—
but none other on that tree.
And on no other tree?

24.

"strange hours"

                "we keep"

That is, our lives.

July–September 1994

Draft 24: Gap

Not under the clarity of the perfectly black square
    articulating pure erasure
where time or speech be emptied under the power
    of a power, the pwer precisely to quadrant the square
and indelibly to color it, acquiring points and promotions
    to higher pwr for the (dark) neatness and the (darker) lucidity
and the (darkest) completeness
    of the orderly achievement of erasure
(in our time),

but a thread
    twisted tensile yet sprung unweavable
a seam
    breaking inside existence
a vent
    that flanged

through dark, and between
  a wander, all awander
    fracture and hinge.

One asks for meaning
    and, faced with any bit of fleck along the crack,
is eager: is it
    in that spot, can one care
for it, is it there?

Now is the now. No matter what. No readiness
for its ungrouted forms.
Meaning is in its lack and in its bet,
in trips that trigger rime.

Let these be called the (underwired) "chips
    of messianic time."

Then: Let coat collections for the cold. And what
    sleeveless passages are, what tunnels
        iced by neon
trudged,

      steps echoing among statistics, and what
wanderers are,
          between hold and hole
                among the mille-letters' shifted marks.

     Who sits at the table when policy is set?

The girder amid, within, among, above
over, on   as if   I had been shot in the head   that day
between   the rickety boards, the middle of city nowhere, in
    construction, before visiting   the locked ward
sight-reading the interface   when the   potential antagonist
at the innermost court   did not strike.   Or so they said.
    Did not yet strike with full intent. Dd nt, or strk
        a never (mean, a nerve), the   deep never
                of the river   of parallels.

                Inside the wish the thick walled house
is useless.   No one can date blankness   Can one
from distant fragments turning   date it, the numb
    greyland gunmetal drypoint?   count fissure as vision?
             number nullus?

Shadows of the lost, can one want to touch the lock,
siphon the lack,
and push that door a little crack? or not?

Frenzied with mere pinholes of opening, letters
      flooded into the space like paint
        and soaked the site
            with unreadable stain. But nothing
heroic, nothing but
tacky shadow piles of
nous and nouns,
not irresistible, but chronic,
set among a greyish fog so deep one cannot compass where one is,
in the lost and found
of aphasia, which makes such wwords you never heard
and pain to hear,
such periphras "that thing you know, like uhh uhh uhh, what
you do that with"
or "with that"

that plunge us further into the irreconcilable.

Was there a choice?

    The specific densities
    of what happens or follows. As it
    does, it does.
    Unfolding gentle garlands of sound,

    little phases that went nowhee

    not a random place,

    but a shadow face.

Unsayable, unsolvable—the whole is built on them.

The dispersion of letters across everything one touches
as if thousands of pages
were only prolegomena
to itself.

The question
              just of "r."
                  Dead, or dread,
it marks the distance
              that the particulars scatter,

which if attended
              would mire the watcher
                      in unparalleled mourning.

              For "historical dead"
   is what   she wrote, but I   split down the selfsame question
              had written "historical dread."

      Therefore there is no volta,
writing being mired forever, or whenever, in its own
inky letters,
      missing and present,
           winding and unwinding,
segmenting indefinitely,
              error, placement, gap, and spell.

Some now more voiceless side is even there,
   as maybe dropp a letter from your name
      but which one should you,
           ache l?

October 1994–February 1995

Draft 25: Segno

Memory makes twins
    from single rocks.
        Similars that materialize
maybe a little
    behind the other,
        one walks the path
bound into forgetting
    and suddenly stumbles on a rock.

Twin from a single
    amnesia,
        grainy speckle of granite,
each and every tittle
    a mirror to double
the forgetting
    "what cannot be spoken."

What cannot not be spoken
    deep in one letter or the other
        bits of line or angle
making now into not:
    this being the t/w of poetry,
        the veery space for shifted marks.

Mourning, risen on the cusp
    of the squandered, doubles
the unhouseled wanterers
    with their unleavened shadows.

To articulate each teacup,
    acorn play plate or play food, each
        child in dress-up, a gypsy, a witch

they were; they were
    foreign and distant what I mean is
        near and constant

drained, a vapor

flares.

No matter who was walker,
    who was not,
        all moved along the toxic
path shrouded in silence
    twigs bound up in ragged canvas,
        fuel incipient.

Could hardly
    put foot down and lift it to the next simple
        for one foot dragged the other's dread.

Dread of the children falling,
    dream saults over the precipice.
        Dead! says the voice, and one
wakes up
    miming her death as "dead"
        within the dark space of action.

Thereupon said: "they spun, swung
    me over the side of the precipice to fall.
        I fell, concrete wall
fell fall,
    down withal
        to the litter of children sent before.

And that was I, forevermore."

The dream-eye behind the real eye
    tenses up,
        anticipating impact.
The dream-speech of the dead
    reverberates, a tunnel of echos
        in a regress of implication.
There was absence stalking déjà vu called
    jamais vu, in which what
        now should be
            familiar, is not.

Of living in a landscape whose flaring cries
    are not sound, are
        cries not to be cried
but atmosphere, ache and el,
    their world-renowned interface

to be remembered as such.
    A task deep within restlessness.
        And thus the story, o

the story—

a twist of the die in the hand,
    a hiss of luck, and they're off!

The claim that for "I" or "you"
    would come the substitute
        "lamb" or "ewe."

Yet in effect it was
    "you" snarled in the barbèd site
        who burned in place of "I."

Luminous globule of redgold poised on the tip of the pipe

blown   blown   blown   a blaze of thinnest glass   in fire broke.

Who then can (now) (or not)
    think like a lyricist
        the wood thrush warble,
those hidden nesting tones
    the leaves that piping whistle
        hist to every whisp,
though it all does exist—
    the round earth hanging
        a dewy blue-green leaf
in the space whose amoral pressure
    and whose whole elements
        engage me like a gear.
I am spun whirring
    and can say no more.

———

Erratum.

There is, however,
a continous addendum
in the name of Erato, muse or must,
livid and singed with signs;

mine posing moments of gloss
on the text of loss
that has long been set
and has been set long:

one conjuncture of ash,
one girder of smoke,
hovering, still,
over rubble also of smoke.

May 31, 1995–July 31, 1995

Draft 26: M-m-ry

        That the airy opening hung somber,/ that the moon
trapezoid/ on the floor be thus, be/ here,
            that musical/ logic in
    the hypnogogic space/ come waves rush/
              crosswise, athwart they
suspend opaque/ particles, sand
         versus translucence,/ and that this
filled/ void, this exfoliated down fold, volatile,/ asks for "rachel
               back,"/ in subjunctive
    sentences/ within the earth's inward
narrow crooked lanes/ and startles who, or what, that
    with me/ tripped the limen and was caught/ Here,
        maze of a maze, the/
          she and I, the I/ of she "back from where"/ were
dazed amid the real/ world, the real real world/ inside which
this "guaranteed destruction/ of papers and files" exists;
      happens as such/ the service
        advertised that this company provides.

We have reviewed / the document—a one-Page Memor-/
    andum— Plastic ribbons blown/ blowing on
      the twisted/ twigs
        of 1995 be any
tree/ by any roadway, every day,/ the
         wish will flood/ such shredded flags of loss/
            and have determined
the variable/ space, feather, point, gleam, spume,/ midge
    streaks readable or not.
    More than that?/ *that it cannot be declassified/*
          dim dawn-long day, twi-grey/ mostly
I just marvel/ at mild blue
      watercolor/ light
        a struggle/ between voices that compete/ to
    identify what I want/ and other voices/ whose
      high twists cannot be/ remembered
    or released in segregable portions./ It must be withheld
that spoke/ of a hand erasing/ across the mind collective/
        hope in the photograph/
          she did not look like herself/ she said/ tho she did

        she'd half forgotten/ what we did, we did
                        all that/ two decades whited out/ static
        "that short/ of a time." *in its entirety /*
        on the basis of the (b) (1) and (b) (3) exemptions of the FOIA.

It's just time/ a soft unreadable light
                        sweet/ wax in wane./
        Poetry the opposite:/ it's always given out/ the fact
                that it remembers forever,/ good at deigning
        memorial design:/ this pile-up of letters—
                        don't do me/ any favors,
                since, as the site/ of detritus and forgetting,/
        one could not want to see it bettered.

        An explanation of these exemptions/ is enclosed.

                        Raise and lower the frames/ to lock
                jacquard./ Aubergine robes, filmed
        herself thus clad,/ ghosts of the homeless/ at the windshield.
Lives/ in furrows unspellable/ mnemosyne misty over
        the field (misspelled/ as filed), its empty/ dashes
declare a signing gap, singing/ gap of herself hello again
                        unpronounceable/ mnemosyne:
        blanking out in extreme/ sadness, bartering/ liquidity
                to hyphenate the cracks/ because
        they mark/ a bridge to
                        particulars one wants "forever."/ Marjoram
                the tiny. Hyssop the twirly. Basil/ the tangy
                                in time stuttering
                        mn-mn-mn-/ cold morse/ dash dash
        and sputtered out, the guttering flares/
                        gone ash.

This is a velocity of signs.

Small yards and all that infrastructure lying bare, beating still.

Train bridge, boulevard razor wire, resignation wholesale.

The many moons of Jupiter and other parts in a kit, the universe

soft in our hearts, who go the road of the unsayable

under phosphorescence, the stars and planets made little

enough for us. Here.

On her cake the "e" in "years" got smudged. Two full

dreams to catch the train

just left. Could barely decipher

the veering of half-spoken, stubs

of the uncanny outcropped along the track,

dead and living yoked together that harrow

shattered shadows and dim light, their immeasurable

desires indignant for name.

Take it all as a loss.

Begin anywhere.

August–October 1995

Draft 27: Athwart

1.

There was an other side
    a space behind, in back,
an overmuch, an
        into which
where muffled voices throb without their names.
      It, whatever the term,
    falls out of range
        such regular registers
as corporations,
    justifications,
            orchestrated bailouts—
        basically, what computes.

Screening odd stuff curled in the can
    all of it strictly rushes,
    it showed drive, but drifted into derive,
    hardly a "ray focusing"
        anything to a point,
    hardly
        what needed to be considered.
    Cheerfully "now," a callow vector,
with the before missing, the after inconsequent.
    Twenty years here,
        twenty there
           flare
        and go frail.

2.

Unsolicited mourning
        floods this site
    a well of muted consciousness.
        Connaissance inutile.
            Do you make it *useless knowledge*?
    helpless
        understanding?
            or *unthinkable recognition*?

Untranslatable it
    is the transverse torque
        across this course.
  A lost specificity:
        not documentary, not song,
but a wall;
    "the" evoked, but what's to point at—
        incomprehensible zero space?
        the ledger's incalculable underside?

An execution usually "over there,"
    some last words that
        frame the poisonous cavils
of the general listener
    who modifies and justifies
who disclaims and denies,
        but basically can't stop
          going along.

3.

Next day, cyclonic rains,
    from which the tree,
an oak of sixty feet
    and sixty years, fell down.
    A tilted force pushed through the winds of ferocity.
Its final muffled noise and muted rush
        were quick,
          a surprise how reverberant,
        how hard to assimilate.

          Ragge of verse
    buffeted by high roaring
            deep
        negation, hole/hold can sometimes split and pivot,
    can create subjunctive hope and affirming rhetorics
          that it may be protected! so provide
        a giant hand to dust tree off and root it deep again!
      from flake to shape remake irrevocable time!
    Give us a shallow dent of dirt in which to prop!

>   There was a time
>   up thru November 10
>   wherein the tree
>   just was, its oakish life
>   as such.
>   One storm and
> one thud. It's the work of a moment.
>   An "event."
>   Something live from the winds
>   that empties "is"
>   of its simplicities
>   and pours "it" as libation on the ground.

4.

Within the concert of the known
    an errant sort
        gets thrown, whereupon
    largo twists itself
        into capriciousness.
The event lists,
    for the soloist,
inside a labyrinth of forgetting,
    can not fake it any longer.
    His hands fall athwart.
His memory has emptied.

    The lapse looms large adrift
belongside what should have
        been unquestionable song.
    Its cumbersome shadow
        blots a round of Mozart.
            His hands lift from the piano.

The others strung with visible notes
    their lyric loops of light
        and kept the music going on
            about the absent sounds.

But they too stopped
    by the empty site
        and had to drop

one upon one, at the deepening spot,
        and fall with him.

5.

The social world, they said, "drained
Is writing the bringing of justice? from the work" after
Is just light   the "conventional
justice?   icons of the 30's,"
        the "standard fare
compromised.   of the time." Quote "in
        1940, when he began
        to spend summers in Martha's Vineyard,
the social world drained from his work." Unquote.

6.

Narrow market-casting
    is meant to prevent
        feeling much, even any, of this.
    It sutures us to things
we will buy
    whatever, straight thru time
        and never look at shame. The process
has been graduated
    in the dispensary, has been stuffed
        with a fine calibration of insistence.
Ambient desires, flavors, and crunchy patenting of colors
        can tell their demographic riddles
to those with ears to harvest the nuances.

And the autumn wet and drear?
the blood-dark leaf?
the button fallen on the street, some "useless scrap its power"?
The flowering pear that
    went its route, a ruddy green, then full, then red, then gold
then god, then golem-brown, its planet balls of rust that
starlings eat?
        Ghosts. Ghosts of ghosts at the open fosse.

November 1995, February 1996, June–July 1996

Draft 28: Facing Pages

      That sense of blockage at the limen
          translating as this word:
            "corruscation"
            must have begun with a thing,
    with rust
         or with metal twist, yet
              I can't remember having seen
     anything, in the split second of
               never known time as such
  among the dream. In deep unwake, it
       was given out as having occurred,
          as being here;
              whereupon blockage
         emerged directly as a word
   created by dispersals among feeling and shadow.

     Invisible scenes and sounds untraced, where
       I feel the dog now dead nudging my elbow
        to get out, the black
fur heart mark on her soft white side, or
query a particular puzzle of this tricky site:
     "did my mother die or not?"

      As for "**corruscation**" as a word,
         there are tapping tactics used to
break it into cor, to rus, rust, corridor
         the turns, transposing word parts, double
     facets vocab. and idio. Nuance the unspoken.
           Not to ignore the relation to "limen"
         as "blocked." Bears a look-see.
     But who actually can bear it?
          the door resisting entry.
          the depth defying surface.
          the shadows telling stories.

The word got spelled with a double "r,"
    which was what I first off
  took this sign to be:
      "corrosion,"

　　　　　the wearing away, dissolution
　　　　gnawed into eaten and eating
　　by the shadowy baby mirrored back
　　　　hinge pivot inside the space. Yet was closer to
　　　　　"**coruscate**,"
　　　　and indicates flashing, glittering,
　　　　senses of light intermittent and vibrant,
　　　　　misted phosphorescent ground.

This dreamed-out "**corruscation**,"
　produces glitter and rust together, transposing each
　　　moment of reading cross the language fonts in that
half-light of coincidence, lush chaos of luck, of lurk the very
　　twist or strew of "be" and "here";
　　　in the log of the **half-life** —
back from where? the shadowy randomness,
　　　　　the sort or sors that throws flat down the die;
　　　and in the **third half** lug, with a laugh, third half—
pulling hard between, punching
　　thru bricked-up spaces, to uncover lintels
　　　for doorways, for doorwas, into which one goes
　　　　　or thought to step
　　　　　　　but tripped the limen
　　　　　　　　　and got caught.

　　　Wild wild wind and wider blow
　　　　　　　　dark violent sky
　　　　　　　trees' greeny heave flags inside out
a twisting quadrant, leaves
　　　　　turn recto verso, twin and flip the facets
　　both a wilderness and not, filled and not
　　　　　　dead or not,
　　　　　　　the chance of seeing or not,
　　later finding or not.
　　　　　　The crisp the whispy cast the
　　　crust of language
　　　random twisting
　　　wet direction the tumbling storm
　　　　　　　soi-distant
it angels right across the narrow page
　　　　dark implacable obsidian
and washes grey green waterthick light
　　　　　over pre-echoes.

70

            The double face of leaves
leaving across the third.
        Second does the first. One is first, one follows.
            Then there is a nother. An e rrancy.

        Post-storm light flat and coral flood front
            over a house
strange in the language
        with "intransitive verbs followed by transitive circumstances"
and mini-gestural adjustments of letters
                losse for loose
                filed for field
                think and thing
                now and not
        those "powerful little berries"
that show that anything could change anything, as we hang here at the
        Earthen door
    inside readiness.

Speckles the foxglove
among stumps squandered into lumber,
        dewy the ragweed over the cumulous waste upbuilt,
            rusted out of factories on the urban corridor,
this is the least of it.
        "Poem" is nothing in the face of this.
    Can not write for a stark seeing, beyond an end point,
        a tip point, over that threshold we have tripped,
    quasi-baffled, singing out our little song "whoo whee."

Which is how I account for the trouble at the heart of poems.
Hard to mark arousal to a justice deferred,
easy to show a joy sometimes too patent,
that very joy deferring justice
with its own desirable pleasures.

Therefore one can only continue word to word,
word to work, picking thru the vanity of any poem, airy, in
                    day light season time motion cloud
        the circumstances of its composition
                wherein the lurid boundary of color,
                    the room where it is written
        form, rhetor, lumen

the disturbances of the poet,
> thought that comes unbidden
>> showbread in the tabernacle
> rising as the poem
>> unfolds itself, offering
>>> the deep and sometimes desperate trouble
>>>> bred at the heart of poems.

That despite the above wants wwords
wsords LEMON on the page
words' letters, lemen sword
so concrete and intimate, so oil-acrid right
stubbly border where yellow
zest on the cirque
shades to pulp and white.

That because of the above
wants something so "os"
the skeleton of yearning ossuarial, wants
implacable "cold ashes"
placed precisely on the non-dimensional edge
> where underside meets recto/verso,
>> a third space

>>> made inside the under and through the shift,

>> the cusp of facing pages

> at the spot between here and there

>> between definite poem

> and the wavy registers

>> from untranslated sensation,

>> untranslatable narratives,

>> shadows and their shadow words.

>> This is the situation:

>>> isolate flakes, randomly settled

ashes that fell being showbread's yeast

a smudge between here and there

no one will understand

this, may be nothing, anyway,

in the face of it.

April–June 1996

Draft 29: Intellectual Autobiography

ck ck ck ck cic
scattered samenesses, in as many
directions: to the sky along the gravel
by the window
through minute
inner slips and other clicks: fast and slow,
light and dark, spectre and color
yes and no

chk, quick
amid disparate axes
dispersing

unsolaced.

    ∧

Song of a traveller about to depart.
Song of a returning traveller.
Fancy named warbles, coming and going,
aprobaterion, epibaterion,
whatever.

The gap—a readable
white line of nothing, a drag
weighting the turn—was just lead.

And what happened in that in-between space, was it
technical   kerfluffle   named   rewards   flatness?
Describe your artistic achievement to date.

    "Baffled, I prepare for even greater foreignness."

    ∧

Outline the traditions
in which you would place
your work.

Aureate
    dismantling sundry.

Then
> the reverse.
Any Old How
> was the pattern.
(Au petit bonheur
> in francophone.)

Little words,
> worming into incipience.
"The a."
> Then, half-contrary,
"a the."

> ∧

Bilderverbot.
> The moon trapezoid on the cool floor.
> Be that way!   Dreamatis personae.

> ∧

Words ending in -ette.
> Kitchenette. Dinette.
Luncheonette. Laundromat. Hopper. The cold air,
vedette, that the poem breathes
tries to warm it by "o muse."

> ∧

Dora Maar photographed Meret Oppenheim's "Déjeuner en fourrure."
> The saucer cup and spoon pic-nic de fétiche, saucy,
> > un grande crème, cum Chinese gazelle
> > tropes roughly everything

then, about 23 years after,

"when Yves Klein began to paint with girls instead of brushes"
> a pretty good idea given everything
whole lithe sweep of them,
> the attraction would differ.

Thus
"*compelling any writing.*"

> ∧

Briefly locate your current project
and state how you plan
to use your time.

Prix fixe, pixillated
strata of culture to dig
out, mote by mote,
where the strabismic lens of any shard
stops me dead.

Immerginated raptures
      are unsung (so to speak) because the word
      doesn't exist
the word for what we are being led to
in the way of
flattened dialectics
in the articulation of joy despite
and within
the crisis—of burning it all off, the whole earth
ripped out,
the pillar of smoke
visible
as we follow, blankly,
the logic of complexity
in which we were raised.

    ∧

Where is the place to stand to say this,
got any syntax would make it clearer?
While we all nickel and dime it
with normal exchanges—are there
    recalibrated tenses
        for conjugating bafflement in modes
           tuned to micro-twangy scales of resistance,
    are there ruptured agents
        for the over-extended job-lost lack-luster
        X? Anyway
I read some words I wrote, I sound like well-meaning
    translations, just slightly unidiomatic, just off,
by a
kindred foreigner
looking stolidly at the spot
citizen of I-am-not-sure

what.

   ∧

"Home, family, illness,
mucus,
childhood,
transitional objects,
household detritus"

thereby

   ∧

hearth heart
(h) (h) (h) (h)
my hear
(th) (t) (th) (t)
   ear
   m'ere
   tereu

   ∧

Trio midge ant caddis
Luminescence keying
pulse of *the* pleasure
watching *a* registr. ways *it*
suffuses

his jay bounces into the lower branches, thick blue beauty.

   ∧

Will have already
begun to play
long tones
long tones on the saxophone
to hear the overtone series
over and over;
where segments mount and narrow
to follow waveses' vibrating dispersal
to observe reverberations in and of the body,
long tones and overtones
in the long time.

   ∧

Georgics, or Work.

"Work!
work! work!" George yelled
at the aspirant. "You'll have to work
hard
like everyone else."

       ∧

What are your methods? Your response
may be general or specific,
but please limit your comments
to the space provided.

Leaves torn from old notebooks
and mildewed subscription blanks   establishing
on the cut-off margins of newspapers   the mouth(er)-eaten
                                                                           writer.
There are pink scraps, blue and yellow scraps, one of them
a wrapper of Chocolat Meunier
dark bitter, no doubt.
Eat clay cuniform for pica, chew spitballs of paper,
snack cartouches
the wilds of stark   SERVING
at the center of the banal   WRIT.

       ∧

What are the directions
you plan to pursue in your work?

Nicht mitmachen

There was a second bomb, not to forget it.

During Auschwitz
after Auschwitz
        not enough prepositions and adverbs for this:
nach Auschwitz, to towards in relation to according to
noch Auschwitz, still still still
        for this, and for this.

So chortle under the stark curse
you entitle "Adorno's verse."

∧

No other world but here.it.is.all.
now.here, all world nowhere
else
the bush, that bush, scarlet
ferocity
flares whenever one catches
sight of this, for
whatever we understand as such
"we are debarred from providing
any indication
whatsoever

that we are inconsolable."

∧

Given, as well, attacks on positions of opening
                      orphic trek back pack little speck

        exposed on that escarpment

Pneunomena

of the status que, we are object cases

in "real time." What looked like a Bad Register

in print. our lives smudged. off-ink. blurred. caught wrong.

we had wanted more hope.

∧

Where
"it literally rains little songbirds"
warblers, orioles, tanagers, flycatchers and thrushes
drained is to become a golf course
specially written into a House bill

∧

Wet snow clumped
words, clumped and melted
lacy pivot points with ice dipped into the
strange cold heat of praxis,
in a white wet storm, and ruffles up its dark
truncated rigging—
some coracle, some jot on wheels
rolls the present through the potlatch
humming its way along
a single spot of ground
into a sinking patch of time.

∧

Propose a work, the work, a work of enormous dailiness, vagrant
responses inside the grief of a century. Pain, of suspicion, of care, the
deformative, washing and cutting that occur
dilatory, minute
in cataclysm, can't help it.   The small time.
Propose
staring at all you know some of it, what cannot be represented
per se
but just exists, in the backwash of gesture
forgotten,

that is forgotten every day

without, and within, memory.

December 1995, June 1996

Draft XXX: Fosse

Imagine a book, a little book,
    whose words are covered
        one by one
with the smallest pebbles—
        fossils imprinted, shale splinters,
slag and gnarls from fossick,
        cheap sweepings arrayed,
a road of morse lines
    step by step
        down the page.

It looks like poetry, runs along depths
    on the surface, slugs
        of a text that is lost;
the instruction it offers
    is delicate,
        maybe misplaced.

The words and their syntax
    come
        not to nothing
        (for the lover of pebbles)
but to an irradiating splayed out
    Something
        so large
it can only be
    marked thus:

+ It could say erosion of the book.

    The pace of the traveller
slowed along the Hansel-Gretel highway,
    given bits of scrap and cornbread
that innocent birds go after, given shiny pebbles
    far too pretty for the story.

The easy exit does not exist.
The circumstance offers more.
She had laid that trail to have it get effaced,
    in order to be abandoned
    to the scrub of a dark wood.

+ It says erasure so cunningly,
    mimics little words
        (flat pebbles),
brings them all to the *a*
    or to the *the* of "be."
        Can choose to investigate.

+ The wordless words
    behind the blocked out words
can be more compassionate than
    the word.
The pebbled lines are filled with otherness;
With only the speech of the stone,
    they gain in empathy.
Reopen pity.

+ Deep ditch, road cut, folds of rock
propose a book of the unraveling voice
incapable and swamped
in the same time as the self.

There is a modulation of feeling
"set myself this meditation"

impossible

project

    barely $\begin{cases} \text{ready} \\ \text{reading} \end{cases}$
to begin.

        •

Imagine a reader, who would resist
      and not resist—
Lightning flashes
      hot silverline domes over the mountain—

resist each word
      even the long night of characters, actions, choreography
which reenact her plundering defiance, resist
      and still articulate the gloss,
      the implacable sweetness
of the Stone.

Narrative sections contain instruction, include
statements about underpass and loophole
do this, do that, listen, do not
disobey,
invest yourself beyond yourself
for you are
a representative of fire
in the windy hopeless cavern, a spark
unable to warm the dark but able still
to see its flaring cries

even
without light, able
to clasp the mists of loss.

There is a space, a ditch
      shallow along the contours of earth
            this bumpy knoll or that hillock
but deep enough to cover
      whatever
            for a couple of years,
until it worms out
      its readable shard,
            its hoops of unforgiveable bone.

Here to imagine the reader
marked by another ring of mark a / a \
  makr, all that morganlongne daag dawning, of
{ the mist
{ the missed

for a meniscus tension of exhumation
swells the page—
$$\text{fugue and segue, modicums of } \begin{cases} \text{wonder} \\ \text{wander} \end{cases}$$
for the $\begin{cases} \text{locus} \\ \text{logos} \end{cases}$
all along the shifting $\begin{cases} \text{boundary} \\ \text{bounty} \end{cases}$

•

Childrenhad gottenup to the attic
hadtaken the boxedmemor
abilia and begunto strew
discovery
       the past became
clutter upon clutter.
   There was no order, no size, no year;
       emotional response was totally mixed.
      What turned up,
what had gone, where by accident something
was into another box. . . . And the book
   of photographs no longer
      fits here, once it was looked at,
         thereupon put, or push, or pull it into, or
out of there. Thus the random recovery
   of unresolved tidbits
can never be assimilated.
   This is the condition of time, going forward athwart
no matter the "gifts" of shame, fantasy, and memory,
   no matter the organic strangeness
of irreversibility.
      This is the condition of time
stuck all over (Merzhouses of Tyree Guyton in Detroit)
with debris of
temporalities gone
      (Merzhouses of Tyree Guyton bulldozed)
   nothing and everything
    plaster-faced dolls,
    plastic tops from margarine tubs,
    tin tea trunk

outcrop

along strata of ever-disjunctive

folds, and smash.

      •

Imagine it
    without the rhetorics of pity
        but not pitiless,
O ruisseaux, o bull of gold and
    lapis, the tongue
        blue lapis
thick with lyric and wine,
    caught in bosky lute trees
caught for song, for song;
    the charm that licks your ear,
Bos Voice
    webbed one way round with strings
        and wound by
linen and pegs. To hold.
    Pressured against. The wood
and sinews gut bound
    leaned into the plectrum
like a figurehead
    drenched by rose.

The bull plays within himself
    at the heart of the labyrinth.

Can visit him dead
bask in his anger and the dirty light
of poetry
and try it all again
astir, that
trenchant call across the fosse
to activate
something
        is it prophecy?
        is it instruction?
        is it mourning?

Whatever the genre,

let it "pass thru its own answerlessness."

    •

  Go stony book

  Step across

  Embrace the wraithe

not as demanded in foundational comandment

nor as refused in annihilating compleynt

but just in the course of things

casting oneself to the same winds.

June–July, 1996

Notes to the Poems

Draft 16: Title. The ledger books with nipples, by Dorothy Cross, from an installation called "Power House," Institute of Contemporary Arts, Philadelphia, 1991, consisting in part of fourteen logbooks, cast wax, and steel bolts. "I am bourne...": Shelley's "Adonais." "Blurred and breathless," citation from *The Odyssey*, Book Eleven as translated by Robert Fitzgerald. Muthoplokon: the word by Sappho. The translation "myth plucker" from a poem of Ben Friedlander helped me on the way.

Draft 17: Unnamed. The citation from Bakhtin ("poetry depersonalizes 'days'...") is from "Discourse in the Novel," *The Dialogic Imagination*, p. 291. The line about "facts" is Michel Leiris, *Manhood*. The long citation, slightly modified from a news article headlined "Lithuanians haunted by Holocaust," was written by *Philadelphia Inquirer* staff writer Fen Montaigne, and appeared July 27, 1992, on the front page. "Reasons to wonder," by Robert Storr, from DISlocations, a show at the Museum of Modern Art, New York, October 1991-January 1992. Memories of Rilke's *Duino Elegies* persist, here the ninth.

Draft 18: Traduction. This poem arose from my being translated into French at the Fondation Royaumont in October 1992, by a group of French poets and writers including Emmanuel Hocquard, Yves di Manno, Jean-Paul Auxeméry, Joseph Guglielmi, Françoise de Larocque, and Joey Simas, as well as Marcel Cohen, Esther Tellerman, and others. The first line was "given" by MM. Antoine Ségovia and Philippe Mairesse (in a special envelope also at Royaumont) to provoke any one realization of the(ir) conceptual art piece "par le Menu" "oeuvre dont les acquisitions et les présentations successives *modifient* la forme." The line "face aux grands enjeux du siècle" is from a review by Yves di Manno of Eliot Weinberger. Fragments as "conspicuous oracles" is Sollers on Mallarmé. "More unstructured, wicked problems" is a citation from John Nosek of Temple University's Computer and Information Sciences. Some of the "nomadic occupation" sentence is by Robert Storr, again from the show called DISlocation, and speaking of David Hammons. With thanks to Micheline Rice-Maximin, Serge Gavronsky, and J-P Auxeméry for checking (or signing off on) my use of French.

Draft 19: Working Conditions. "The traces of each successive handwriting regularly effaced as had been imagined have in the inverse order been (regularly) called back." Thomas de Quincey, "Suspira de Profundis." "Virile piety" is a phrase by Charles Derr, poet. Quotations about music are either by pianist John MacKay, program notes for Luciano Berio and Yusef Lateef, or from program notes on Joan La Barbara's vocal performances. "so I had a feeling tonight that nothing..." are three lines from David Antin's "scenario for a beginning meditation," in his *Selected Poems*, p. 144. "Not boiling to put pen to paper/ Perhaps a few things to remember—" is Zukofsky, *"A"* 1. "During my long nights...": said by V.Y. Mudimbe, African philosopher and poet, about fratricidal conflict in Rwanda in 1961, and quoted from the *PEN Newsletter* 81—Writers and Human Rights in Africa—(May 1993), p. 4.

Draft 20: Incipit. The material in italics draws on, but alters, lines of "First Dedication" in Anna Ahkmatova's "Poem Without a Hero," *The Complete Poems of Anna Ahkmatova*, translated by Judith Hemschemeyer (Boston: Zephyr Press, 1992), 545. This Draft is the beginning of the first fold; it corresponds to "Draft 1: It."

Draft 21: Cardinals. "But with Schönberg, affability ceases." (Adorno, *Prisms*, p.150). "Ghost pieces," come, as in Draft 19, from program notes for "Jacob's Room" by Morton Subotnick. "Studded with acquisitions ...and layoffs." (Bruce Barber, The New Museum, brochure.) "On Foot I Made My Way Through the Solar Systems" is a short poem by the Swedish-language, Finnish poet Edith Södergran; I have cited the first three lines in modified form and extended the poem. The text on which I based myself is from Södergran's *We Women*, translated and introduced by Samuel Charters, San Francisco, Serendipity Books, 1977. "A disorder of memory" echoes a title by Freud. The "encyclopedia" citation comes from *Writing Beyond the Ending*, p. 102. Continuing the fold, this Draft corresponds to "Draft 2: She."

Draft 22: Philadelphia Wireman. "The Philadelphia Wireman sculptures were found abandoned on a side street in Philadelphia on a trash night in 1982.... The entire collection totals approximately six hundred pieces and appears to be the creation of one person." It is surmised that the person is dead, because the objects were thown out en masse. It is surmised that he was strong (i.e. male) because the thick wires seem to have been twisted without the help of pliers or other tools. And it is surmised that he was African-American because of the particular Philadelphia neighborhood in which they were found and because of the tradition of Kongo power objects on which these works seem to draw. The summary from Janet Fleisher Gallery, Philadelphia was written by John Ollman. "Traumscrapt" material from Linda Kauffman, *Special Delivery*. "Cursive scrimmage" from Alan Shima's description of Beverly Dahlen in *Skirting the Subject*, p. 129. Some descriptors throughout from Ann Jarmusch's reviews and stories of The Wireman's works in *ART News* and *The Philadelphia Inquirer*. Other descriptors, and list of items or objects used for the multi-media works by the Wireman from Janet Fleisher Gallery. All these descriptors and lists have been broken up and augmented. For the tradition of nikisi (pl. minkisi), the instruction to "randomize the flow of paths," and the question (actually applicable to a Kongo tomb tradition) "Can you tie up the anger of the dead?" see Robert Farris Thompson, *Flash of the Spirit: African and Afro-American Art and Philosophy*, pp. 222 and 134. This Draft corresponds to "Draft 3: Of."

Draft 23: Findings. I was reminded of ways of organizing time in Evitatar Zerubavel, *The seven-day circle: the history and meaning of the week*. Lee in section three is Lee Hickman, the much-mourned editor of *Temblor*. Evocation of the "Angel or the Power" is from H.D., *Sagesse*. "O baby" is a citation from Big Bopper, "Chantilly Lace." "Wet rails and the oil of crushed leaves" is SEPTA's explanation for late trains in autumn. The cricket paraphernalia at the Nelson Atkins Art Museum in Kansas City, Missouri. The "wee keeps" in section 17 by Bill Walton, Institute of Contemporary Art exhibit called "Conversation Pieces," June 1994, Philadelphia. Words in the last section are from William Carlos Williams, "January Morning." The reader might already have surmised that each section of this poem both enacts an hour of the day and also refers or alludes to the prior Draft corresponding to its particular number. The Draft also corresponds to "Draft 4: In." "Findings" is thus doubly folded.

Draft 24: Gap. The citation from Benjamin, "Theses on the Philosophy of History" (as at the end of Draft 12: Diasporas) and the girder from Reznikoff are clear enough. There are also unmarked words from Garrett Stewart, Hank Lazer, Colleen Lamos, Victoria Harrison, and Uwe Kraemer. I also use, with thanks, a 1994 review of *Drafts*, in which Caroline Bergvall gave, as my phrase, "historical dead" instead of "historical dread." Thereupon I include a number of intentional typographical errors in this work, whose title is the same as "Draft 5: Gap."

Draft 25: Segno. The doubled rocks were inspired by (but don't develop quite the same as) the work of Vija Celmins called *To Fix the Image in Memory* (1977-1982), consisting of eleven different real rocks set next to their uncannily identical replicas made by Celmins of painted cast bronze (ICA, Philadelphia). "Squandered" from Ingeborg Bachmann: "Or could he [Wittgenstein] mean that we've squandered our language because it contains no word that can touch upon what cannot be spoken?" *Songs in Flight: The Collected Poems of Ingeborg Bachmann*, trans. Peter Filkins, xxi. Girder/rubble, as before: Reznikoff/Oppen. See Draft 6: Midrush.

Draft 26: M-m-ry. The poet Rachel Tzvia Back is a former student of mine. "The earth's inward, narrow, crooked lanes" comes from Donne, "The Triple Foole." "The real world..." is Carl Rakosi. "We have reviewed the document," and so forth, in italics: a letter from that governmental body overseeing the administration of the Freedom of Information Act. See Draft 7: Me.

Draft 27: Athwart. "Conaissance inutile" is Charlotte Delbo's phrase about knowledge gained in, and by virtue of, the Holocaust. "Ragge of verses" is Donne. "Useless scrap its power" is Eliot Weinberger on Cecilia Vicuña. The citation about the artist is from a *Times* review of Aaron Siskind (as in Draft 14). See Draft 8: The.

Draft 28: Facing Pages. "Intransitive verbs": the writer Charles Bechtel. "Powerful little berries": First Nations people about the glass beads of Venice traded to them. "Showbread": Exodus 25: 30. "Circumstances of its composition... disturbances of the poet" and subsequent phrases (modified): from Peter Quartermain, a paper on Robert Duncan. "Cold ashes": Ingeborg Bachmann, as in Draft 25. See Draft 9: Page.

Draft 29: Intellectual Autobiography. I had been composing Drafts for ten years, for they began in early 1985; Draft 29, harkening also to Draft X: Letters, was written as an anniversary work. The list of genres from Scaliger, *Poetices*, 1617, cited by O. B. Hardison. Grant application language cribbed from the usual suspects. "Baffled..." is a self-citation from 1985, one of the initatory recognitions. Dora Maar's 1936 photograph, along with Lisa Liebmann's citation (p. 126) about Yves Klein in Bice Curiger, *Meret Oppenheim*. "Compelling any writing": LZ, "Mantis: An Interpretation." "Work": GO—an incident appropriated from a friend. The citation about "household" art is slightly altered from Faith Wilding, "Monstrous Domesticity," M/E/A/N/I/N/G 18, p. 7. The saxophone—a description of the childhood of LaMonte Young, based on *The Philadelphia Inquirer*, Nov. 28, 1995, F4. Some of the forms of paper that Dickinson used, described by Mabel Todd Bingham in *Bolts of Melody*, xii-xiv. Nicht mitmachen—an ethics of resistance in Theodor Adorno, from whom also the mote as strabismic lens and the challenge to post-Holocaust poetries, "nach Auschwitz...." "That we are inconsolable," from Nicolas Abraham and Maria Torok, *The Shell and the Kernel: Renewals of Psychoanalysis*, p. 130. "Raining songbirds" a citation from David Hankla, a field supervisor for the U. S. Fish and Wildlife Services, in a news article, Nov. 27, 1995, *The Philadelphia Inquirer*, A4.

Draft XXX: Fosse. The little book does, in fact, exist. By Ann Hamilton, in a private collection. Included are muted, unmarked, or vaguely signaled citations from Louis Zukofsky, Armand Schwerner, *Beowulf*, Donald Rackin, Ezra Pound, and John Felstiner on the Paul Celan/ Nelly Sachs correspondence. See Draft 11: Schwa.

POTES & POETS PRESS PUBLICATIONS

Bruce Andrews, *Executive Summary*, $9.00
Dennis Barone, *Forms / Froms*, $7.00
D. Barone / P. Ganick, *The Art of Practice: 45 Contemporary Poets*, $18.00
Martine Bellen, *Places People Dare Not Enter*, $8.00
Steve Benson, *Reverse Order*, $9.00
Paul Buck, *no title*, $8.00
O. Cadiot / C. Bernstein, *Red, Green & Black*, $8.00
Abigail Child, *A Motive for Mayhem*, $8.50
A. Clarke / R. Sheppard, eds., *Floating Capital*, $12.00
Norma Cole, *Contrafact*, $10.50
Norma Cole, *Metamorphopsia*, $8.50
Cid Corman, *Root Song*, $7.50
Beverly Dahlen, *A Reading (11-17)*, $8.50
Tina Darragh, *a(gain)2st the odds*, $8.00
D. Davidson / T. Mandel, *Absence Sensorium*, $14.00
Jean Day, *The I and the You*, $11.00
Ray DiPalma, *The Jukebox of Memnon*, $8.50
Ray DiPalma, *Provocations*, $11.00
Rachel Blau DuPlessis, *Drafts 15-XXX, The Fold*, $12.00
Rachel Blau DuPlessis, *Drafts 3-14*, $9.50
Rachel Blau DuPlessis, *Tabula Rosa*, $8.50
Theodore Enslin, *Case Book*, $8.50
Norman Fischer, *The Devices*, $7.00
Peter Ganick, *Rectangular Morning Poem*, $9.00
Michael Gottleib, *River Road*, $10.00
Jessica Grim, *Locale*, $10.00
Carla Harryman, *Vice*, $7.50
P. Inman, *Think of One*, $7.50
Melanie Neilson, *Natural Facts*, $10.50
Gil Ott, *Public Domain*, $8.50
Maureen Owen, *Untapped Maps*, $9.50
Stephen Ratcliffe, *spaces in the light said to be where one/ comes from*, $9.50
Kit Robinson, *The Champagne of Concrete*, $9.00
Leslie Scalapino, *Goya's L. A*, $8.50.
Leslie Scalapino, *How Phenomena Appear to Unfold*, $9.00
Spencer Selby, *House of Before*, 9.00
Ron Silliman, *Lit*, $7.50
Ron Silliman, *Toner*, $9.50
Diane Ward, *Imaginary Movie*, $9.50

Potes & Poets Press also publishes A.BACUS, a
single-author newsletter, eight times a year; a series
of Limited Editions, called Extras; and, has some back
issues of its earlier chapbook series.

Please write to us at:
Potes & Poets Press Inc
181 Edgemont Avenue
Elmwood CT 06110-1005
for a complete catalogue and ordering information.